W9-DGF-523

With Colors Flying

Highlights of the American Revolution

Marguerite Buranelli

Illustrated with paintings by

John Trumbull

Crowell-Collier Press · Collier-Macmillan Limited, London

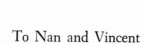

To Nan and Vincent

Contents

Introduction

John Trumbull, 1756~1843

John Trumbull was one of America's first soldier-artists. He was born at Lebanon, Connecticut, in the middle of the eighteenth century. His ancestors were English; his family prosperous New England merchants.

Young John attended the local grammar school where he studied the usual subjects of the day, Latin, Greek, Religion. He continued his education at Harvard University and was graduated at the age of seventeen. His first position was that of schoolmaster at Lebanon, but with the outbreak of the Revolution he joined the militia. He became adjutant of the first regiment of Connecticut troops. The regiment marched to Boston in time to witness the Battle of Bunker's Hill. Years later Trumbull remembered and recorded its fire and fury.

The young soldier had always liked to draw. Now his skill was put to the test. General Washington needed a plan of the British works at Boston Neck. Trumbull volunteered for the mission. In the face of gun and cannon he crawled through enemy lines to draw a map of the fortifications. Shortly after completing his assignment, he was appointed the general's aide-de-camp. He held the post for only a few weeks but remained in the army, serving with distinction in New York, New Jersey and Rhode Island. He reached the rank of colonel before resigning his commission in 1777.

Trumbull "put aside cockade and sword" to pursue a boyhood dream. He would become an artist. He worked alone for several years teaching himself the rudiments of painting. Later he journeyed to England to study with the celebrated American artist Benjamin West. West's London studio was a Mecca for fledgling Rembrandts. There they learned sketching, sculpture and oil painting. They copied the old masters, noted the various techniques and styles and went on to develop styles of their own.

Trumbull's apprenticeship was interrupted by an incident harking back to his military days. It concerned the British spy Major John

Detail. The Battle of Bunker's Hill. Yale University Art Gallery

André. André had recently been captured by the Americans and executed at Tappan, New York. In retaliation the English seized the ex-Yankee officer and sentenced him to a prison term. Trumbull spent seven months in jail. On his release he returned to Connecticut but was soon back in London, once again a pupil of Benjamin West.

West was a historical painter whose "Death of General Wolfe" was highly regarded. Under his influence, Trumbull found himself concentrating more and more on scenes from history. This led to the project that was to become the guiding force of his life. He decided to record on canvas the great events of the Revolution. From the Battle of Bunker's Hill to Washington's resignation at Annapolis, the pictures would capture for all time our heroic past. They would serve as a memorial to the men who gave their lives in the name of liberty.

Trumbull was well suited to the task. An excellent artist and former soldier, he was close to the men who had led the struggle for independence. His father was involved in politics as well as business and had served several terms as Governor of Connecticut. His two older brothers held important posts in the Continental Army. George Washington, Benjamin Franklin and Thomas Jefferson he counted among his friends. It was in Jefferson's Paris residence that Trumbull began the sketches for "The Declaration of Independence."

For over forty years the patriot artist worked on what he called his National History Series. Six of the eight pictures were painted in London. Though far from the scene of battle both in time and place, Trumbull was determined that every detail should be correct. Uniforms, weapons, flags must be authentic. For "The Declaration of Independence" he traveled up and down the eastern seaboard seeking out and sketching the signers of the momentous document. He did not put down his brush until their likenesses were as true as he could possibly make them.

Trumbull painted these pictures to be engraved, with prints sold to the public. In this way he was able to retain possession of his work and still realize a certain profit. Also, he made replicas of four of the canvasses for the Rotunda of the Capitol in Washington.

When he was seventy-five, "the old Colonel" gave his paintings to Yale University in return for an annuity or pension. The next year a museum was built to house the remarkable collection which has been kept intact to this day.

John Trumbull was *the* painter of the American Revolution. No other artist and no other historical period are so closely connected. It is through his eyes that we see again the great events of the war. Faithfully recorded, alive with dash and color, the epic scenes are an important part of America's priceless heritage.

Recruits Against Regulars

The Battle of Bunker's Hill

All night the men had been digging. Quietly under cover of darkness they wielded pick and shovel tearing holes in the flinty ground. They worked fast and expertly for they were farmers and knew how to clear the land. Rocks and tree-stumps soon disappeared, and the men began to build a sturdy earthen wall. By dawn a good sized fort had taken shape on the hilltop, its gun platforms facing Boston Harbor.

As the work neared completion, General Israel Putnam of Connecticut rode up on a white horse. He stopped to talk first to one exhausted soldier, then to another. After the night's labor, uncertain of the trial ahead, the men were in low spirits. They needed encouragement, and Old Put, his reputation for bravery going back to the French and Indian War, could inspire even the greenest recruit. He told the men they had done a fine job on the fort. It would give the British second thoughts, he said. They'd see that the Americans intended to defend their rights. And if they chose to fight—why, colonials could stand up to regulars any day.

But looking at the weary band he must have wondered if amateurs *could* stand up to professionals. The men didn't look very military. Few were in uniform. Most wore everyday farm clothes—homespun shirts and leather trousers, woolen stockings and cowhide shoes. The King's men, on the other hand, would be well turned out in trim scarlet jackets, white breeches and regulation boots. Their weapons, too, would be different—colonial muskets versus British rifles. An unequal contest, the

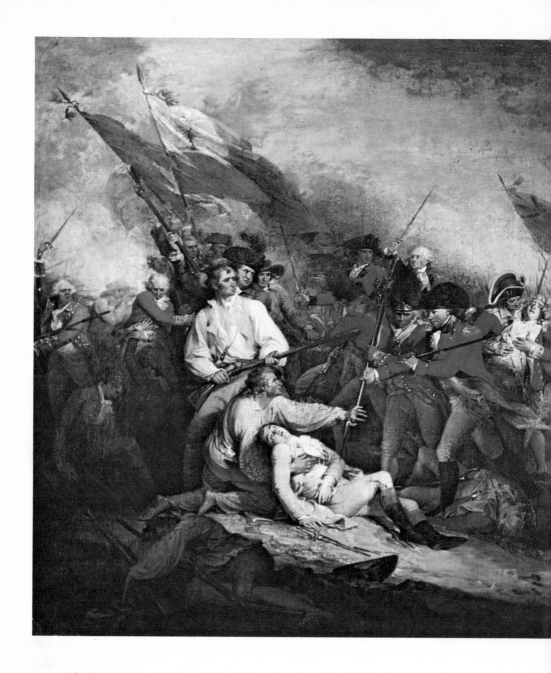

general had to admit. With troubled thoughts he wheeled his horse and rode off along the dusty road.

Meanwhile, Boston Harbor was coming to life. As the watch changed aboard *H.M.S. Lively,* the morning lookout glanced idly shoreward. Puzzled, the young sailor looked again. Through the haze he saw a strange sight. Yesterday the hill opposite the harbor had been covered with nothing but tall grass and rail fences. Now there was a fortification of some kind. Quickly he reported the situation. His su-

periors were not too surprised. It was June, 1775, a time when anything might happen. The city of Boston was occupied by the King's army, but it was a city under siege. Since the clashes at Lexington and Concord two months before, the British regulars had been penned up in town. The surrounding countryside bristled with opposition. The colonial militia, their headquarters in nearby Cambridge, could be seen parading along the roads, massing on the village green, drilling, marching.

Detail. The British officer, Major John Pitcairn, was mortally wounded during the Battle of Bunker's Hill. Yale University Art Gallery

Sir William Howe, second-in-command of the British forces, found the situation intolerable. He decided to act. He would break the siege, attack Cambridge and capture the ammunition depot there. After that, the Americans would surrender. The rebellion would be over.

Through their spy system the colonists learned of the plot. To prevent the redcoats from breaking out of Boston, they decided to fortify the ground overlooking the harbor. A place called Bunker's Hill was mentioned in the order, but by some mistake Breed's Hill, half a mile away, became the site of the fortification. A smaller redoubt or fort was erected on Bunker's Hill, and that is the name history has given the opening battle of the American Revolution.

As dawn brightened the eastern sky the battle began. The *Lively* opened fire on the Americans. Other ships in the river readied their cannon. The first shots were aimed low; they burst against Breed's Hill and did no damage. The naval gunners quickly corrected their mistake. Soon the shots were hitting the target. They crunched against the rude walls of the fort, ricochetted along the parapet. British land batteries joined the bombardment. Volley after volley thundered across the water.

The militiamen were startled. Working on a nearby entrenchment, they threw down their tools and ran for cover. Inside the fort they crouched, unnerved by the sudden attack. Their fear mounted—and with reason. Farmers-turned-soldiers, they understood the plow better than the cannon. They were very young, many still in their teens. This was their first taste of war. They saw their comrades hurt and bleeding, watched helplessly as they fell to the ground.

William Prescott, a veteran officer from Pepperell, Massachusetts, tried to reassure them. Though he held the rank of colonel, he took his place side by side with the men. This was true of many other officers that warm June day.

Prescott told the men not to panic. There was work still to be done. Besides, what were a few cannon balls? Not one in a hundred ever did any damage. To prove it, he sprang up on the parapet and walked its length. Sword in hand, a dauntless figure in a three-cornered hat, he strode back and forth in the morning sunshine. Shells burst about him. Any one of a dozen might have struck him. He never flinched. The cannonade grew stronger. Prescott ignored its fury, ignored the rain of shells. See how close they come to hitting me! he seemed to say. Then he leaped from the wall to the cheers of the men. With no further ado they went back to work.

The day wore on. The barrage continued. It was early afternoon as Joseph Warren, a young doctor from Roxbury, took his place near the redoubt on Bunker's Hill. Warren was president of the Massachusetts Provincial Congress. He need not have been in the field at all. He was there purely from choice. Earlier, in talking with a friend, he had stated his feelings. He said that when untrained amateurs are asked to face seasoned professionals they deserve all the support they can get. For this reason he wanted to fight along with the men. Wearing his finest clothes, he went into battle.

By now the regulars were free of their trap. General Howe and his crack regiments had already left Boston. Boats and barges ferried them across the river. The British troops reassembled on the beach not far from the two fortified hills. With drums beating, bayonets catching the last rays of the sun, they began to move forward. Light infantry, grenadiers, marines, they made their way to the foot of Breed's Hill. Slowly, calmly, the long red line moved upward.

On the crest of the hill the colonials waited. They numbered a thousand to the enemy's two thousand. William Prescott was among them, fearless as always in the face of danger. John Stark was present with his New Hampshiremen, also Thomas Knowlton and the Connecticut militia. Still on horseback, General Putnam wove in and out among the troops. "Don't fire until you see the whites of their eyes," he barked. Even as he gave the order, he wondered if it would be carried out.

The wave of scarlet came closer and closer. The enemy advanced to within a hundred yards of the works. Still the Americans waited. Then, suddenly and at the just the right moment, they opened fire. A crash of musketry, a cloud of smoke, a burst of flame. Frontier marksmanship paid off. The redcoats were forced back. Dazed and bewildered, they ran toward the boats. Amid the fury Old Put gave a sigh of relief.

General Howe's feelings were quite the opposite. Watching from the beach, he couldn't believe his eyes. The rebels were better than he had expected. He sent to Boston for reinforcements, then massed his men for another try. The second attempt was as disastrous as the first. Once again the regulars were overwhelmed. They fell back to the water's edge.

Again the scarlet troops began to march. Boldly, fearlessly, they surged up the steep hill. Their third attempt succeeded. The militiamen had little ammunition left. Working all night, fighting all day, they were tired and hungry. Fresh troops had not arrived from Cambridge as planned. Resistance was no longer possible. The British swarmed to the summit and attacked the fort. After deadly hand-to-hand fighting the colonials were forced to retreat.

The redcoats didn't spare Bunker's Hill. With equal fury they fell upon Dr. Warren and his men, defenders of the redoubt. The Patriots fought bravely but it was a one-sided struggle. A handful of provincials against a hundred Englishmen. Bare fists against bayonets. Recruits against regulars. In spite of the odds, the young doctor refused to surrender. Bullets whizzed through the air as he sought to rally his countrymen for one last stand. Turning to call to them, he was struck in the back of the head. "He died in his best cloaths," a British officer wrote, "every body remembers his fine silk-fringed waistcoat."

Joseph Warren's sacrifice was not in vain. His gallant effort and tragic death strengthened the Patriot cause. The people were more determined than ever to defend their rights as free men. The battle itself inspired them further. They could not claim victory, but they could

8

claim something equally important—the knowledge that they had stood up to British regulars. Citizen soldiers had pushed back the best troops of the strongest nation on earth, not once but twice.

The courage and fortitude displayed at Bunker's Hill had more than local effect. News of the battle spread from Maine to Georgia. It gave the people new hope. "We have a fair chance of throwing off England's rule," they cheered, "and some day forming a country of our own."

The Declaration of Independence was no longer just an optimist's dream. Soon it would be a reality.

Detail. Lieutenant Thomas Grosvenor of Connecticut and Peter Salem, his servant, were among the militiamen who fought to defend Bunker's Hill. Yale University Art Gallery

Meanwhile, the Second Continental Congress met in Philadelphia. The members appointed a commander-in-chief of the Army. The honor went to George Washington of Mount Vernon. It was an excellent choice. Washington was a veteran soldier who had fought in the Indian wars. He was a man of sound judgment, courage and integrity. A Virginian, he would unite the country north and south. England would realize that this was more than a local uprising led by a few Yankee radicals. It was a struggle of all the colonies.

Early in July the new commander arrived in Massachusetts. He immediately began to recruit and train a full-fledged army. Volunteers flocked from remote hamlets and bustling cities, from farms and villages, eager to serve under him. At the outset and all during the war General Washington enjoyed the loyalty and devotion of his men. They would have followed him anywhere.

The main objective during the summer of 1775 was to drive the British from Boston. There were other plans as well. One concerned Canada. How would the pendulum swing in that great land to the north? Most of her inhabitants had fought—and lost—a war with England. Many were still bitter about the defeat. Perhaps they would go against the Crown, side with the colonists in their bid for freedom. Congress decided to find out.

Two armies were sent northward. Colonel Benedict Arnold and a thousand hardy frontiersmen marched from Massachusetts. They made their way through the Maine wilderness, along the Kennebec River and the Chaudière,

"To the Storming We Must Come at Last"

The Death of General Montgomery in the Attack on Quebec

then pushed on to Quebec. A similar army under General Richard Montgomery set out from Fort Ticonderoga in New York State. Montgomery advanced to Montreal where he captured the garrison. From Montreal he followed the St. Lawrence River to Quebec. Outside the great walled city the two leaders joined forces.

It was then the end of December, a cold blustery afternoon. General Montgomery paced the floor of his makeshift headquarters. Since early in the month he and his men had been encamped on the outskirts of Quebec. Arnold's command was not far away.

"To the storming we must come at last," mused the general. Glancing out the window he could see the spires and turrets of the city and the great stone wall behind which the enemy waited. A frown darkened his brow.

The tall fair-haired officer was tired of war. Born in Ireland of well-to-do parents, Richard Montgomery had served with honor in the British army before joining the Americans. A true patriot, a firm believer in the cause, he nevertheless longed for peace. He hoped to settle the Canadian question as soon as possible and then return to his New York farm.

If only the French people had come over to our side, he thought. If only the British commander had accepted our flag of truce.

It was wishful thinking. The French remained loyal to England. The British commander refused the rebels' flag. Sir William Carlton would not surrender the garrison. Much as he disliked the idea, Montgomery realized there was nothing to do but take the garrison by force. And, he decided, by surprise. A dark and snowy night would cover their movements.

Even as his thoughts took shape, the sky seemed to darken. The general noticed the change. It began to snow. At first a few flakes, then a steady fall. The tiny crystals beat against the casement windows and settled on the wide stone ledge. They covered the distant rooftops and the great rugged cliff known as Cape Diamond. A full-scale blizzard had begun.

The general summoned an aide. Young Captain McPherson sprang to attention.

Colonel Arnold was studying a map of the city. By the fading light he traced the various land and water batteries. The Gibraltar of America, he thought, a natural fortress. No wonder the British feel safe behind its walls. And there they intend to stay. They won't come out and fight, so—sooner or later—we must go in.

The colonel rose to light a lamp. Drawing the blinds, he saw some snow flurries against the evening sky.

Benedict Arnold lives in history as a tarnished hero. Late in the Revolution the dark dynamic officer became a spy for the British, a traitor to his country. At the time of the Canadian campaign, however, he was a brave and loyal soldier. On the long journey northward he shared with his men all the perils of the wilderness. Cold, hunger and fatigue plagued their every step. They waded through icy swamps. In small boats they crossed turbulent rivers. They struggled through tangled growth and plodded through snowdrifts. Many became sick and died. Some deserted. Before long the expedition was reduced to half its size. The survivors kept going. After eight grueling weeks the valiant band finally reached their destination. One of the most difficult marches in military history had come to an end.

On a bright November day Arnold and his command crossed the St. Lawrence to behold at long last the majestic cliffs of Quebec. Gazing upward, the colonel from Connecticut had but one goal—to capture the fortress at the summit, to force Carlton to surrender. Arnold knew the job wouldn't be easy. But then, the past weeks hadn't been easy, and the army had managed to come through.

Bent over his desk at headquarters, the colonel pondered the strategy of his attack. To storm Quebec at any time would be an achievement. To storm it in winter would be a miracle, and the commander who succeeded would be a hero indeed. A victory at Quebec would bring him fame and glory.

Just then there was a knock at the

John Trumbull

The Death of General Montgomery in the Attack on Quebec

Yale University Art Gallery

14

Detail, facing page. Among the volunteers under General Montgomery's command were, from left to right, Major Return Jonathan Meigs, Captain Samuel Ward, and Captain William Hendricks. Detail at right depicts "Colonel John Lewis," Chief of the Oneida Indians. Yale University Art Gallery

door. Arnold looked up as Captain McPherson hurried into the room. He brought a message from General Montgomery.

The two armies had come to Quebec by separate routes. Now they would attack the city from separate points. Montgomery was to proceed along the pass between the base of Cape Diamond and the river. At the same time Arnold was to advance from the opposite end of town. The two forces would meet at a central point, attack the main gate and take the city by surprise. Such was the plan. It was wild and daring. With luck it just might succeed.

Montgomery thought it would. With a feeling of optimism he assembled his New York troops, seven hundred in number. Silently they marched along the dark, narrow pass. On one side was the ice-bound river. On the other soared the towering heights of the palisade. At the summit stood the British garrison.

The night was bitterly cold. The wind howled through the leafless trees. It stung the men's faces and numbed their hands. It penetrated the thin fabric of their worn and ragged coats. In spite of the ordeal the columns pushed onward. Higher and higher they climbed.

Presently they came to a barrier. A roadblock of bushes and fallen trees had been thrown up hastily. Carlton was expecting them. The Americans lost no time in tearing down the obstacle. Their leader didn't stand idly by. Working along with the rest, Montgomery hurled the branches out of the way until the road was clear. The march could go on.

Here the troops hesitated, uncertain of what lay ahead. Noting this, the general turned and called in a firm loud voice, "Men of New York, you will not fear to follow where your general leads. March on, and Quebec is ours!"

His words were like magic. The troops fell into line. They continued along the steep and winding road. The storm grew worse. Icy blasts went bone deep as the men slipped and stumbled and groped along the precipice.

Suddenly they saw it. Out of the darkness appeared a building. A blockhouse stood some yards above them on the side of the hill. Was the place occupied? Was there a sentry on duty? Were the guns in the loopholes manned? A scout went forward to find out. Noiselessly he approached the rude wooden structure. He stood and listened. Not a sound came from within. He waited a moment longer, then signalled to his comrades. The troops leaped forward. With Montgomery in the lead they advanced at double-quick time.

A report crashed through the crisp night air. The blockhouse was guarded; the guns were manned. The British soldiers on duty had no intention of letting the Yankees pass. The first shot was followed by a second and then a third. The volley continued. Montgomery was hit three times. Beyond help, he sank to the ground. Young Captain Mc-Pherson was killed also. At the end of the attack twelve Americans lay lifeless in the deep snow.

Stunned by the death of their leader, the remaining troops scattered. They raced down the hill. They never reassembled or continued the march. They never combined forces with Benedict Arnold.

Arnold himself was badly wounded as he tried to carry out his part of the plan. In a skirmish at one of the gates a musketball tore through his leg. Many of his men were killed or taken prisoner. Morale among the survivors was low. Even so, the colonel refused to admit defeat. He stayed on in Canada for several months waiting for a second chance. The chance never came. In the spring, when the river was again open for navigation, England landed reinforcements to defend the city. The cause was lost. Arnold realized this at last. With the remnants of his army he retreated to Lake Champlain.

The assault on Quebec was a failure. The strongest fortress on the American continent would stay in British hands. Canada would remain part of Britain. Even so, the inspiring heroism of Richard Montgomery should never be forgotten. The courage and perseverance of Benedict Arnold should receive its due.

The Case
Against the
King

The Declaration
of Independence

The Canadian campaign was a disappointment. The Americans were discouraged by the defeat. Where they failed in Canada, however, they succeeded at home. The moment he took command, General Washington intensified the siege of Boston. He fortified the surrounding heights. He tightened the blockade. Seven thousand redcoats were virtual prisoners in the city they sought to occupy.

The next step was to drive the British out of Boston. To do this Washington needed guns. He immediately thought of Fort Ticonderoga. The fort, three hundred miles away in New York State, harbored a supply of captured cannon. These guns would save the day. "No Trouble or Expense must be spared to obtain them," Washington declared. He gave the assignment to Henry Knox, a former Boston bookseller. Knox was more than equal to the task. In the dead of winter the energetic young officer transported forty-three cannon over snow and ice and through miles of often trackless wilderness. At last his "noble train of artillery" reached the army at Cambridge. It was an engineering feat marveled at even now.

Early in March the Ticonderoga guns opened fire on Boston. The cannonade continued for three days and three nights, forcing General Howe to evacuate the city. The British army sailed from Boston harbor never to return.

Washington had reason to be optimistic. But there was cause for concern also. New York was open to attack. The whole East Coast was defenseless. The general turned his attention southward.

Now was the time to see to the welfare of the whole United States.

More and more, Americans were referring to their country as the United States—a free and independent republic. After a year of war they no longer felt that their differences with England could be resolved. The quarrel could not be patched up. A complete separation from the mother country was necessary.

In the spring of 1776 the Second Continental Congress again met in Philadelphia. Delegates from the thirteen colonies assembled there to discuss the many problems confronting a people at war. High on the list was the question of independence.

"Now is the time," urged Sam Adams of Massachusetts. "We must delay no longer." In the State House on Chestnut Street he addressed the delegates. A firebrand ruled by his emotions, Sam Adams had one goal —separation from the mother country. During the past decade his every effort had been expended in the case against the King. Popping up here and there at town meetings and rallies, he could always be counted on to make a speech or write a pamphlet on this most explosive subject. Tories, as the British sympathizers were called, were his natural enemies.

His cousin John Adams agreed that separation was necessary. Unlike Sam, however, he arrived at the decision only after careful consideration. Short and crotchety, John Adams was a brilliant lawyer, honest and fearless. A man of sound intellect, he relied on reason, never allowing his emotions to cloud his judgment. He was a gifted orator.

"Three million people have the power and opportunity to form the wisest and happiest government on earth." The white paneled council room reverberated with his voice. And again: "Independence is rolling in upon us like a torrent." His fine phrases and clearheaded logic influenced delegates. Many who hoped for a reconciliation with England came over to his side. Many who thought Congress should wait before announcing its intentions began to waver. As a result of John Adams' efforts, a committee was selected to prepare a formal declaration. Chairman of the committee was Thomas Jefferson of Virginia. To him fell the task of writing the momentous document.

Jefferson was well qualified for the job. A graduate of William and Mary College, he had spent long hours studying law, government and philosophy. He was active in the legislature at Williamsburg. He represented Virginia in the Second Continental Congress. Though he spoke little and participated in few debates, he was well liked by his colleagues in Philadelphia. They appreciated his quiet manner and friendly ways. They respected his scholarship.

In a rented house on Market Street, the sandy-haired Virginian settled down to the task. Without book or pamphlet for reference he began to write. As pen flew across paper he sought to mirror the minds of the people. He was not trying to be original. He was not trying to put forth new principles or new arguments but rather to repeat the principles and arguments that had already been thrashed out in public meetings.

Jefferson began by stating that separation from England was necessary.

When in the Course of human events, it becomes necessary for one people to dissolve the political bands which have connected them with another, and to assume among the Powers of the earth, the separate and equal station to which the Laws of Nature and of Nature's God entitle them, a decent respect to the opinions of mankind requires that they should declare the causes which impel them to the separation.

The author next explained the rights of man.

We hold these truths to be self-evident, that all men are created equal, that they are endowed by their Creator with certain unalienable Rights, that among these are Life, Liberty and the pursuit of Happiness.

Jefferson went on to say that the people had long been denied those rights. They had been taxed without their consent; their appeals had been ignored, their petitions refused. He ended by stating that the colonies were determined to be free.

We, therefore, the Representatives of the united States of America . . . solemnly publish and declare, That these United Colonies are, and of Right ought to be Free and Independent States. . . . And for the support of this Declaration . . . we mutually pledge to each other our Lives, our Fortune, and our sacred Honor.

The rough draft took two weeks to complete. It was submitted to John Adams and Benjamin Franklin for approval. Adams made a few revisions. Franklin did likewise. The sometime printer had recently returned to America. For years he had lived abroad trying to reconcile the differences between the colonies and the mother country. He did his best but to no avail. Now the aging philosopher was back in the City of Brotherly Love, a delegate to the Congress.

When Franklin and Adams were through with their corrections, Jefferson made a "fair copy," which was placed before the other delegates. During the better part of three hot, humid days they debated its various points. They struck out a paragraph here, added one there, changed this word or that. They asked questions, made suggestions, agreed, disagreed.

As Thursday, July 4, was drawing to a close the Declaration was formally put to a vote. The huge room was alive with tension. Some of the delegates were grave and solemn as they addressed the chair. Others were worried and nervous. All realized the importance of the stand they were about to take.

When it came his turn to speak, Ben Franklin asked to examine the

John Trumbull
The Declaration
of Independence
Yale University Art Gallery

paper one more time. He scrutinized each paragraph. "Come, come," John Hancock, President of the Congress, spoke with some impatience. "We must be unanimous. No pulling different ways. We must all hang together."

"Indeed we must all hang together," smiled the old man. "Otherwise we shall most assuredly all hang separately."

At last the final delegate was heard. The vote was unanimous.

The document was not signed, however, until the delegates recon-

vened on August 2nd. John Hancock underscored his firm bold signature with a flourish. "There," he said, "his majesty can now read my name without glasses. He can double the reward on my head."

The Boston shipowner spoke lightly, but he realized the gravity of the occasion. A leading Patriot, Hancock was wanted by the British government—and had been for some time. Ever since the days of the Stamp Act, he had worked long and hard in the interest of freedom. He was willing to risk his fortune—his life as well—for what he believed. At the time of the Boston Tea Party he condoned the action of the colonists. Some said he helped throw overboard the obnoxious consignment of tea. There was a price on his head. The crime—high treason. As President of the Congress John Hancock could expect the gallows if America lost the war.

But America wouldn't lose the war, Hancock was confident. Settling back in his chair at the Speaker's table, he adjusted his fine lacy cuffs and watched as the delegates filed out of the room.

The deed was done. In the flag-draped chamber of the State House history had been made. Soon the Declaration would be printed on parchment as a permanent record. Copies would be sent to all the colonies— from the rocky farms of New Hampshire to the tobacco fields of Georgia —from the sandy shores of Long Island to the western reaches of the Alleghenies. It would cross the Atlantic. In London, George III and his ministers would read it and wonder at the audacity of the rebels. Few documents would so profoundly affect the world. In time the Declaration of Independence would be cherished as a charter of freedom. It would take its place as one of the most important documents ever

written.

Astride his chestnut horse, General Washington surveyed the riverbank. He drew his worn cape about his shoulders, while the sorrel moved briskly in the December cold. The afternoon sky was pale and sunless. A light snow had begun to fall, and great masses of ice could be seen floating on the water.

The commander was worried. His army was about to cross the river, and he knew it would be a perilous crossing. Perhaps it was foolhardy to make the attempt, but there was nothing else they could do. They must hit when least expected—and they must hit hard.

Washington watched grimly as the troops moved toward the waiting boats. The men seemed pitifully unequal to the task ahead. They were gaunt from lack of food. Their tattered clothing was scant protection against the freezing temperature. Many were without shoes, their feet wrapped in burlap. Nevertheless they were glad to be on their way. They leaped eagerly into the forty-foot boats that would take them to the opposite shore. Manned by the gallant fishermen of John Glover's Massachusetts regiment, the loaded craft was ready to push off.

A victory at Trenton was badly needed. The past few months had seen little but defeat, and the people were discouraged. Morale in the army was at a low ebb. Enlistments were running out. There was no incentive to sign up for another stretch in a war that seemed all but lost.

Washington had been able to drive the British from Boston, but after taking his army to New York—with

"Victory or Death!"

The Capture of the Hessians at Trenton

the idea of holding the Hudson against British forays to the north—his luck had changed. In the summer of 1776 General Howe and his brother, Admiral Lord Howe, had sailed into New York Harbor. They boasted reinforcements from abroad. The admiral's stout, tall-masted ships held guns, ammunition and supplies—and most important of all, soldiers. Among the newcomers were thousands of foreign mercenaries. Hired from small German states, they filled out the British ranks. Many came from the principality of Hesse. These Hessians were generally well disciplined, bold and daring. They added to Washington's growing problems.

In August the Americans lost the Battle of Long Island. Their retreat to Manhattan was carried out with great skill, but it was nonetheless humiliating. Weeks later the infantry engagements at Harlem Heights and White Plains were indecisive. In November Fort Washington and its garrison of over two thousand surrendered to the British. Fort Lee on the New Jersey Palisades was likewise lost.

Retreat was the order of the day. With the redcoats at their heels, Washington and his bedraggled patriots fled helter-skelter across New Jersey. It was touch and go for some time, but the Americans finally reached the safety of Pennsylvania.

Encamped near the Delaware River, Washington took stock of the situation. The foe held New York City and much of New Jersey. Next they would try to take Philadelphia. If that happened, if the Capital were lost, the Americans might have to withdraw farther south, into Virginia, and from there engage in guerrilla warfare. Washington didn't want that to happen. They must take the offensive now. And the place to strike was New Jersey.

Espionage was a commonplace during the Revolution, just as it is today. Washington put great faith in the system, and one of his most trusted agents was the courageous weaver and butcher John Honeyman. Some weeks before, Washington had sent Honeyman on a secret mission. Posing as a British sympathizer, the itinerant butcher made his way through New Jersey and observed the defenses there. The regulars gave free rein to Tories, and Honeyman was able to penetrate deep into British-held territory. At the right moment he was "captured" by two American scouts and "questioned" by the commander himself. At this interview Washington heard some cheering news. New Jersey, Honeyman said, was badly defended. With the coming of winter the British generals had left the colony. In their place they stationed a number of Hessian regiments. These mercenaries were given the unpleasant task of guarding the cold and desolate outposts of New Brunswick, Princeton and Trenton.

Detail. General Washington was accompanied by his Military Secretaries, Lieutenant Colonel Robert Hanson Harrison and Captain Tench Tilghman. Yale University Art Gallery

In command at Trenton was Colonel Johann Rall. The burly Hessian officer, with his fierce mustachios and swashbuckling air, had no fear of the rebel army. "A few rustic clowns," he jeered in his native German. "They can't whip us." Overconfident, he did little to protect the town. There were no fixed fortifications. Daily patrols were held to a minimum. Drilling was a now-and-then affair. All this Honeyman noted as he meandered along selling his wares.

"Here is our victory," said Washington, and he made his plans. "December 25—at night—is the time fixed for our attempt on Trenton. We will clip the Hessians' wings while they are so widely spread."

The strategy was perfect. What better time to strike than Christmas? There would be much carol singing, wine drinking and dreaming of home. There would be little attention to duty. The result: an outpost open to attack.

Shortly after twelve on Christmas Day the Americans began to leave the Pennsylvania shore. With the blue-coated Marbleheaders at the oars, they pushed off into the icy flood. All was quiet. No one talked. The troops scarcely moved. Surprise was the secret weapon. Their very lives depended on it.

The river was only a fifth of a mile wide at this point, but it was ice-choked and almost impassable. Sleet, snow and gale-force winds added to the peril. Through it all the work progressed. The boats made one crossing, discharged their passengers, then returned

Detail. Major General Nathanael Greene, second from left, was General Washington's second-in-command. Yale University Art Gallery

John Trumbull
The Capture of the Hessians at Trenton
Yale University Art Gallery

for another load. This continued all afternoon and into the night. The watchword was "Victory or Death," a phrase coined by Washington. The men realized the truth of this, for once on the Jersey shore they would be in hostile territory. They must wait there for the remaining troops, then form ranks for the crucial nine-mile march into Trenton. After the Hessians were alerted there would be no turning back for the Americans. They must capture the enemy or themselves be captured.

At dusk Washington and his staff were ready to embark. There was young Nathanael Greene of Rhode Island. One of the war's ablest generals, he was second-in-command. Dark, snappish General John Sullivan of New Hampshire would add his military know-how. Henry Knox was in charge of artillery and horses. His cannon had saved the day at Boston. He hoped for the same success now.

On the opposite shore Trenton was dark and silent. The town's hundred-odd houses were shuttered and still. A lone sentry stood watch at the great stone barracks that sheltered the sleeping Hessian troops. Though far from home, they had enjoyed a lively Christmas celebration. Colonel Rall himself had stayed up late playing cards at a friend's house. In the small hours of the morning he returned to headquarters to get some sleep. He was soon awakened. It was scarcely light when an aide burst into his room with startling news. The Americans were attacking! Somehow they crossed the river during the night and meant to take the town.

Rall couldn't believe his ears. The Delaware was choked with ice. Only a madman would have tried to cross it in such weather. Then he recalled an incident of the night before. A messenger had tried to warn him during the card game. He gave Rall a scribbled note. Rall paid no attention to the warning, just pushed the paper unread into his pocket. Now, too late, he realized his mistake. He threw on his uniform, took up his brass helmet and bayonet and rushed into the street. Cannon balls were whizzing through the frosty air. The Americans were charging from every direction. Taking deadly aim, they fired from behind trees and fences. They crouched in cellars and at windows.

Taken by surprise, the Hessians were too stunned to fight back. All they could do was run—and not very far. They were surrounded. Wherever they tried to go, they were met by a rebel force. General Sullivan and his men commanded the river highway. Nathanael Greene and his brigades were pushing inland along Pennington Road, while Washington held the high ground at what is now Princeton Avenue. Their escape cut off, the Hessians downed arms, surrendered, were captured. The Battle of Trenton was all but over.

Colonel Rall did the best he could, bravely trying to rally his men. In the melee he was hit by a bullet. He fell from his horse and, mortally wounded, was carried to his headquarters. As his jacket was removed, a crumpled note slipped from his pocket.

Hours later General Washington appeared at Rall's bedside. Through an interpreter the victorious American offered his sympathy to the dying German. Rall looked up at the man he had so often wanted to capture. It no longer seemed important. He could think only of his command. He asked that his men be treated kindly. The tall Virginian made a solemn promise, then silently left the room. He walked into the snowy street, mounted his horse and galloped toward the boat landing.

As Washington and his exhausted band rowed back across the river that dark December night, they scarcely realized the importance of their victory. The plan had been to attack by surprise, and the enemy could not have been more surprised. The battle had lasted less than an hour, but over nine hundred Hessians had been taken prisoner. The Americans lost just four men. This confirmed what Bunker Hill only had hinted at —that a citizen army could stand up to well-trained veterans and emerge the winner. And the Trenton victory proved to the country that George Washington was the right man for the job. It gave the people renewed hope and courage in their struggle for independence.

Springing the Trap

The Death of
General Mercer
at the Battle
of Princeton

Around a battered oak table in a lonely farmhouse sat half a dozen rebel officers. A log fire burned fitfully on the hearth. It cast jagged shadows about the room and illuminated the stern features of the men assembled there. John Sullivan, Arthur St. Clair, Hugh Mercer —loyal patriots who had served the cause since the beginning of the Revolution. Their most recent campaign was at Trenton. On that cold and stormy night they had done more than their share to bring about victory. Now, a week later, they were back in New Jersey. Again they were in the field, again ready to face the enemy.

In spite of their recent defeat, the British still held New Jersey. Their fortifications dotted the countryside. For the Americans there could be no rest until they were gone. To drive them out, Washington had boldly recrossed the Delaware. With his tattered regiments he had marched again toward Trenton—and suddenly found himself confronted by a superior British force. Hurriedly he summoned his senior officers. At a council of war he explained the situation. A worn but dauntless figure in blue and buff, he spoke slowly, thoughtfully.

The British were in front of them, said Washington. The river was at their rear. They were in a trap—a devilish trap. For this he could thank the earl, Charles Cornwallis, descendant of an ancient English family. Cornwallis was an experienced officer, one of King George's best generals. Following the Trenton debacle, the earl's home leave had been canceled. With orders to rout the Yankees once and for all, he had swarmed down from New York gathering in garrisons as he went. Now, on the afternoon of January 2, he was bivouacked not far from the American line. The two camps exchanged occasional fire; there was some nasty skirmishing. A full-scale battle could start at any moment— with the Americans on the defensive.

Two courses were open to the Americans, as Washington pointed out to his officers. They could stand and fight. Or they could go back across the river, and retreat into Pennsylvania.

John Trumbull
The Death of General Mercer
at the Battle of Princeton
Yale University Art Gallery

The men pondered the alternatives. An all-out engagement now would be disastrous. The odds were too great—eight thousand well-trained regulars against five thousand battle-weary Continentals. But—the other side of the coin—retreat would be fatal. They said as much to their chief.

The general agreed. To cut and run would be the worst possible thing for morale. It would undo all the good of Trenton. Still, they must act, and fast. They were in a trap and they had to get out.

Detail. General Washington led his men on toward Princeton. Yale University Art Gallery

There was a long silence. The winter sky darkened against the leaded windowpanes; the fire burned low in the grate as the hard-pressed Americans sought to spring the trap.

Meanwhile, across the snow-covered hills, Cornwallis too was pondering a question. From his Trenton headquarters he could see the ragged colonial forces. With their backs to the river, they were sitting ducks asking to be picked off.

Should he strike tonight—the thought was tempting—or wait until morning? He decided to wait. His own troops had been marching all day over muddy roads and sodden fields. They were hungry and tired and in no condition to fight.

34

By morning it was too late. The Americans had vanished. At their council of war they had devised a plan—to get behind Cornwallis' line and march north to Princeton. They would capture the King's regiments stationed in the little college town. After that they would proceed to New Brunswick where the British had vast supplies of food and clothing.

No one knows whose idea this was—perhaps no one ever will—but the plan was a brilliant one, and Washington was quick to adopt it. That was part of his genius.

Before setting out, the general gave orders for a token force to remain behind. They were to stoke the fires, do sentry duty and build entrenchments. In other words, give the appearance of an occupied camp. The ruse was as old as warfare itself, but it worked. The redcoats were completely fooled. There's the prey ready for the kill, they thought, and complacently settled down for the night.

As the British slept, the Americans quietly stole away. With sacking wrapped around the gun-wheels, and everyone pledged to absolute silence, they began the long desperate march. Fortunately the weather had turned cold. The roads, muddy during the day, were now firm enough to support the weight of the cannon. Slowly the army moved along in the darkness and crept past the enemy's flank. Slowly, they pressed on toward Princeton.

Within two miles of their destination Washington stopped. In the icy dawn he beckoned to General Mercer. Mounted on a fine gray horse, Mercer rode forward. He was told to separate from the main force and take the nearby Stony Brook bridge. Washington explained that the regulars in Princeton would probably march out to join Cornwallis. Mercer could foil their plans by seizing the bridge before they reached it. He could check Cornwallis in the bargain. The English general would be after the Americans in a matter of hours.

The assignment was an important one, and Washington felt it was in good hands. He had great respect for Hugh Mercer. He and Mercer had met years before in Virginia. They had been friends ever since. The two officers were very much alike. Both were simple and straightforward, men whose word was their bond.

Mercer, no less than his superior, knew what war was all about. As a youth in his native Scotland he had fought with Bonnie Prince Charlie when the Pretender made his dash for the throne. He saw his brave Highland comrades die on the bloody battlefield of Culloden. Immigrating to America, he became a country doctor—such had been his early education. For years the sober-minded young Scot traveled up and down the frontier healing the sick. At the outbreak of the French and

Indian War he returned to the military. He served under the ill-fated Braddock just as Washington had done.

In 1775 Hugh Mercer enlisted in the Continental Army. The cause of liberty was dear to him. It soon became his whole life. Though no longer a young man, he was willing to make any sacrifice, face any danger, in the name of freedom. Now, as he saluted briskly and galloped off to marshall his troops, there was but one thought in his mind—to take the bridge over Stony Brook, regardless of the consequences. With a brigade of four hundred cold and weary souls, he swung to the left and sped across an open field leading to his objective.

At that very moment a British detachment out of Princeton was also approaching the bridge. Washington had been right: the redcoats were attempting to join up with Cornwallis. Lieutenant Colonel Charles Mawhood was in command. Easy in the saddle, the distinguished-looking colonel might have been a country squire out inspecting his estates. To complete the picture, a pair of spaniels scampered about his horse's legs, dodging this way and that on the frosty road.

As the first rays of the sun brightened the sky, Mawhood reached the bridge and crossed it. Suddenly he spied Mercer's column approaching from the south. His nonchalance instantly disappeared. He was every inch a British officer as he quickly took in the situation. Wheeling about, he raced for the high ground near a Quaker meeting house.

Now Mercer caught sight of the enemy. Like Mawhood, he sought the same high ground—and got there first. From behind a fence his men opened fire. A deadly volley thundered through the morning air, then

Detail. In the melee Mercer's horse was shot from under him. Yale University Art Gallery

another volley and another. The British returned the fire. They charged with their bayonets. The Americans fell back in disorder. Many were raw militia witnessing their first bayonet charge. It was too much for them and they fled in panic.

In the melee Mercer's horse was shot from under him. On foot he tried to rally his men. As he struggled, a British trooper came by clubbing him with the butt end of his rifle. Stunned, Mercer fell to his knees. He was immediately surrounded. Someone demanded his surrender. Mercer refused. Surrender was not in his Scottish nature. He knew he was doomed; still he must fight to the end. In one desperate effort he raised his sword. A dozen troopers lunged at him with their bayonets. He gasped in pain and fell over on his side, mortally wounded. And so the military career that began thirty years before at Culloden ended far away on another bloody battlefield.

Meanwhile, on the road to Princeton, Washington heard the roar of the guns. He ordered forward a detachment of militia which hastened to Mercer's assistance. They were too late to help the general, but his men were heartened by the sight of reinforcements. They stopped in their flight, re-formed their lines and advanced on the British position.

In the midst of the battle Washington appeared. Waving his hat and cheering on the troops, he was an impressive figure on his white charger. Fearlessly, he approached within thirty yards of the enemy. He was now between the firing lines of both armies. An aide, watching the heroic spectacle, thought his chief must surely die. He covered his eyes in horror, but when the smoke of battle cleared, the commander was still alive and mounted, still leading his men.

"Bring up the troops!" he called. "The day is ours!"

This was certainly true. The Americans were in control. They held the field and it was Mawhood's turn to retreat. The red line wavered and broke. The regulars scattered in all directions.

Leaving orders for the bridge to be destroyed, Washington pushed on to Princeton. General Sullivan had already arrived. Together they captured the remaining British regiments. The army then went into winter quarters at Morristown some forty miles to the north. So ended the Battle of Princeton. New Brunswick and its well-stocked warehouses would have to wait, but no matter. There was this satisfaction: Cornwallis would enter Princeton only after the Americans had left.

Cornwallis could do nothing. He knew that as long as the Americans commanded the heights of Morristown, his troops were in danger. The situation was hopeless, and he was forced to withdraw from New Jersey. Washington had accomplished his purpose. In doing so he had executed one of the greatest military manoeuvers of the century. 38

Mix-up in London

The Surrender of General Burgoyne at Saratoga

In the twilight of a summer evening a British spy made his way northward. His cloak billowed in the breeze as he guided his horse through dense forests and shaded woodlands. Spruce trees, oak and hemlock towered on either side of the winding trail. In the distance lay the rolling hills and well-tended farms of upper New York.

The countryside was not unlike his native England, but the man on horseback scarcely noticed it. Intent on his mission, he cared only about the road ahead and the message which he carried in his breast pocket. Written on tiny pieces of paper and rolled up inside a quill, the message was from Sir William Howe. Howe's base was in New York City many miles to the south. The country in between bristled with rebel soldiers, as the lone traveler knew only too well. Recently two fellow couriers had been captured by the Americans and hanged. Still others had been sent out and never heard from again. It was a sobering thought for the young Englishman.

Next day at Fort Edward, on a path by the water's edge, General John Burgoyne was chatting with an aide. The sun was already high in the sky. Its rays fell on the tents and fortifications of the British camp, erasing some of the harshness of army life. There was an air of ease about the place, and the general himself seemed relaxed and happy. He and his army had just completed an arduous march through difficult country. The wilderness was behind them. Its deep forests, ravines and swamps had done their worst, but the men had not faltered. They withstood fierce militia

John Trumbull
The Surrender of General Burgoyne at Saratoga
Yale University Art Gallery

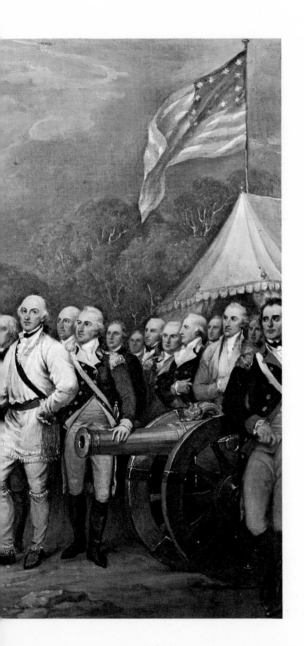

raids. They dodged the deadly fire of snipers who seemed to lurk behind every tree. After weeks of hardship they finally arrived at Fort Edward and now were resting on the banks of the Hudson River.

Resplendent in scarlet jacket and gleaming medals, the general looked out over the water. The Hudson, he mused, that mighty stream which will take us to Albany and triumph. Speaking to the young officer at his side, he seemed more a man of letters than a soldier. This was to be expected. John Burgoyne was a part-time playwright fond of grand language. To him the world was a stage and he liked to strike a pose. With it all, he was a competent general. He treated his men with respect and was sincerely interested in their welfare. For this reason they called him Gentleman Johnny. He was a skilled tactician. He knew how a battle should be fought. It was he who planned the present invasion from the North. It was his Grand Design.

The plan was a good one. With Canada as a starting point, the idea was to advance along Lake Champlain, capture Fort Ticonderoga, proceed south to Albany and seize control of the Hudson River. All knew the importance of that great waterway stretching from the northern wilderness south to New York Harbor. It carried men and supplies from New England to other parts of the country. This mighty river helped to bind the colonies together.

General Burgoyne was not the only commander involved in the invasion. He and his eight thousand mixed British and German battalions would require help. That help must come mainly from Sir William Howe in New York. Sir William was now Commander of the King's troops from New England to Georgia.

According to the plan, Howe and his army were to sweep up the Hudson at the same time as Burgoyne was pushing southward. They were to meet at Albany. The combined forces would then strike a hammer blow at the Americans, who would surely surrender. The Hudson would belong to the British. New England would be cut off from the rest of the country. The rebellion would collapse like a pricked balloon.

So far the invasion had gone well. Burgoyne had left Canada on schedule and captured Fort Ticonderoga without too much trouble. Old Ti was once more in British hands. The Yankees had taken it two years before.

Leaving Ticonderoga, Burgoyne led his men to Skenesborough and then to Fort Edward. It was a regular obstacle course, but they survived to tell the tale. Part one was accomplished. Now they must wait on Sir William. Burgoyne hadn't heard from the commander in weeks. Messenger after messenger had been sent to New York seeking word of his whereabouts. None of the couriers had returned.

Surely Howe knew he was to join Burgoyne's troops at Albany. That is, if London had alerted him. . . But had they? The British capital was three thousand miles away. The officials there sometimes forgot about their troops fighting in America. Burgoyne realized this but assumed there was no reason to fret. Howe was probably whirling his way up the Hudson at that very moment. When they heard from him, they would continue the invasion, cross the river and set out for Albany.

Explaining the situation to his aide, the general stopped in mid-sentence. From the distance came the sound of hoofbeats. Clop, clop, louder and still louder. To the officers standing by the water's edge, it was the most welcome sound in the world. They looked up to see a mounted figure speeding toward them. A hard-riding courier, he had apparently come a long way at top speed.

The horseman recognized Gentleman Johnny and pulled to a halt. He leaped to the ground. Tossing back his dust-covered cloak, he produced the innocent-looking quill container. He handed it to Burgoyne. Then he went off to take care of his winded horse. The young officer accompanied him. Together they walked toward the camp.

General John Burgoyne was left alone to read the most important letter of his life.

"Dear Sir," he began, squinting at the small writing. The message was scarcely legible, but Burgoyne didn't mind. It was from General Howe and that is all that mattered. "I have heard from the rebel army of your being in possession of Ticonderoga, which is a great event. . . ." Burgoyne smiled. Like most people he enjoyed a pat on the back. But Sir William hadn't sent a man two hundred miles through enemy territory just to pay a compliment. There had to be more to the message.

There was. This the general perceived as he read on. "My intention is for Pennsylvania where I expect to meet Washington but if he goes to the northward contrary to my expectations and you can keep him at bay, be assured I shall soon be after him to relieve you. Success be ever with you. Yours, etc. WILLIAM HOWE"

"My intention is for Pennsylvania. . . ." Burgoyne was stunned as he read and reread the words. Pennsylvania! Sir William couldn't mean that! He was supposed to be on his way north so that the two armies could meet at Albany.

What was Burgoyne to do now—go back up the Hudson, retreat to Canada? Should he remain at Fort Edward in comparative safety? Should he go forward and attempt to occupy Albany—with no hope of assistance from Howe?

Albany is on the west bank of the Hudson River. Fort Edward is on the east bank. If Burgoyne decided to go forward, it would mean crossing the river by a bridge of boats. Once they crossed over, the boats would be abandoned. There would be no turning back. They would be cut off from Fort Ticonderoga; cut off from Canada.

Gentleman Johnny had his shortcomings, but cowardice was not one of them. Bold and courageous, he was ever ready to obey orders. His orders were to make for Albany. And that is just what he would do. Without Howe's reinforcements his troops would be greatly outnumbered, but they would do their best. They would not turn back.

And so General Burgoyne and his men crossed to the west bank of the Hudson. With spirits high and bands playing, the troops passed in review at Saratoga (now Schuylerville). Astride his fine horse, Gentleman Johnny swept off his tricorn hat and reminded the men that Britons never retreat. Then they all went into battle.

There were two engagements at nearby Freeman's Farm. History calls these engagements the Battle of Saratoga. The Patriot forces were led by General Horatio Gates. Stooped in stature with thinning gray hair, the general was known as "granny Gates." In contrast, the officers serving under him seemed even more dashing and colorful than they actually were.

The first encounter resulted in a draw. It was a long bitter struggle.

It took its toll of Burgoyne's forces and left them in a desperate position as they encamped on the battlefield to prepare for the next encounter. Two weeks later they again pressed the attack. This time they were roundly defeated, due mainly to the efforts of General Benedict Arnold. Arnold had served gallantly in Canada, and he was no less courageous now. With superhuman energy he flew against the British and won a brilliant victory for America. It was to be his last. He never again fought on the side of his native land.

Burgoyne's army retreated to the high ground above Saratoga. There they remained for over a week, a weary, discouraged band. Outnumbered four to one, they could no longer go into the field with any hope of winning. Their camp was surrounded. Men and horses were being picked off by sharpshooters. Food was giving out.

There was no alternative but to surrender. This they did on October 17, 1777. The invasion from the North was over. Gentleman Johnny's Grand Design had failed.

"The fortune of war, General Gates, has made me your prisoner," were Burgoyne's words. What he might have said is: "A mix-up in London has made me your prisoner." It was indeed a mix-up. Lord George Germain, Britain's colonial secretary, had promised to instruct General Howe to join forces with Burgoyne at Albany. The letter was written but never sent. Somehow it was put aside and forgotten—a very costly blunder. Having no definite orders from London, Howe acted on his own. He set sail for Pennsylvania. Burgoyne was left to face the enemy alone.

The Battle of Saratoga was one of the most important battles in American history. It marked the turning point of the Revolution. From then on Europe began to think better of the struggling little country. France came to her aid. Rich and powerful, she sent money, soldiers and ships across the Atlantic. She promised her full support.

The United States had an ally.

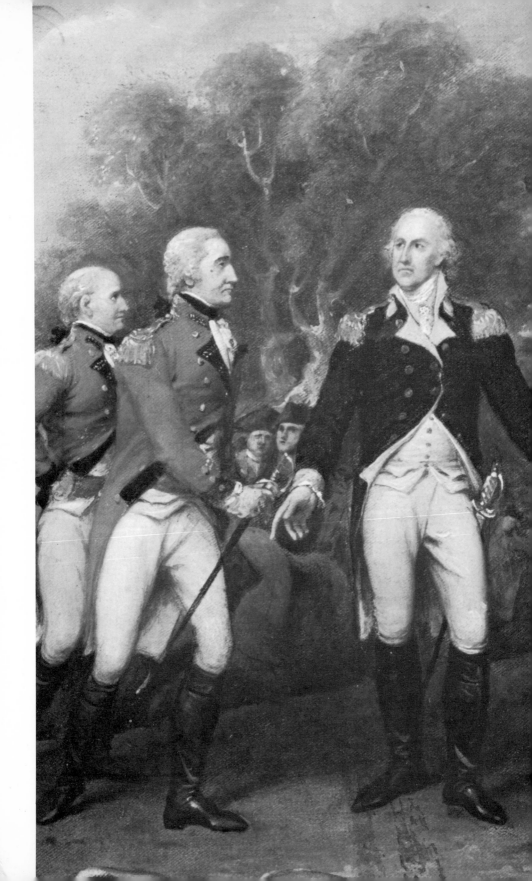

Amid the crash and thunder of battle Lord Charles Cornwallis rode out on a desperate tour of inspection. Mounted on a large brown charger, he cut a handsome figure as he solemnly surveyed the works. Briefly he scanned the horizon—the low-lying Virginia hills, the clear October sky. The morning held promise of fine fair weather, but the commander knew that for him, his army and his King the day would be anything but fair. He had only to see the fallen parapets, the walls riddled with gunfire, the wounded and the dead to realize that all was lost.

In a rude dugout that served as headquarters he conferred with his officers. "What shall we do, gentlemen?" he asked. "Shall we fight to the end?"

The answer was in the negative. Everyone agreed that to continue the battle was pointless. The men had done all that was humanly possible. They were outnumbered five to one and couldn't survive another day's bombardment.

The general acknowledged the verdict and then fell silent. The siege of Yorktown had been long and harrowing. Now it was over. A wave of gloom engulfed him as he realized what he must do. For the first time in his career the proud Lord Charles Cornwallis must surrender to the enemy. Summoning an aide, he dictated a short but historic message. It was addressed to General Washington encamped nearby.

The Sound of a Single Drum

The Surrender of Lord Cornwallis at Yorktown

Sir, I propose a cessation of hostilities for twenty-four hours, and that two officers may be appointed by each side to meet at

Mr. Moore's house to settle terms for the surrender of the posts of York and Gloucester.

The letter on its way, Cornwallis dismissed his officers and tried to relax. He had been up all night. He was weary and discouraged. Loosening his starched collar and unbuttoning his scarlet jacket, he sat for some moments deep in thought. Where had he gone wrong? How had he got penned up in this wretched little town, with the circle becoming smaller and smaller, the noose tighter and tighter? The questions raced around in his mind as the morning wore slowly on. Suddenly he looked up. He listened. The noise of battle was dying down. Soon it had ceased altogether. In its place could be heard the sound of a single drum. A lone British drummer boy, high on a parapet, was signalling a truce. Then all was quiet.

It was a dismal ending to what might have been a brilliant campaign.

After Burgoyne's defeat at Saratoga just four years ago, the British determined to forget the north for a while. They would concentrate on the south, which should be easier to subdue. The key to the south was Virginia, or so Cornwallis thought. The Old Dominion was the richest colony and one of the most populous. It supplied the American army with men, money and food. Conquer Virginia and you have won the war. It was an exciting prospect for the ambitious earl.

During the spring of 1781 he and his army trooped through the green Virginia hills. They sparred with the Patriot forces led by the Marquis de Lafayette. The young French general, though highly capable, was no match for the veteran Englishman. Cornwallis more than held his own. August found him about to enter Yorktown, to fortify the little harbor city and then continue the campaign.

Situated on the York River, Yorktown had once been a thriving tobacco port. Trading overseas with England, it was the busiest on the Chesapeake. Now its best days were past. It was neglected and run-down. Business had come to a standstill. The population had dwindled. In the ordinary course of events the place would have sunk into oblivion. But events were not ordinary, and when Charles Cornwallis led his army ashore on York peninsula, he gave the dying town lasting fame.

The earl's first order of business that hot summer day was to locate suitable headquarters. Always a man of taste, he chose one of the few really good houses in town. Next he made plans to fortify and defend the peninsula, with ramparts and redoubts constructed at strategic spots. Across the river lay Gloucester Point. Here too he would erect defenses and station a detachment of infantry.

His second-in-command, General O'Hara, had not yet arrived. Cornwallis took time to write him a note: "Dear Charles: After a passage of four days we landed here and at Gloucester without opposition. The position is bad, and of course we want more troops. . . ."

If additional troops were wanted at the outset, as the summer wore on the need became desperate. In mid-August a large enemy force began to march south from New York. George Washington was in overall command. Under him was the Comte de Rochambeau and his well-trained French regiments. The French had been in America for a full year. This was to be their first combat mission since leaving home, and they were determined to do a good job. France must shine in their glory.

For Washington, too, the journey held special interest. He was anxious to capture Cornwallis of course. The noble lord was too good a general to have walking around free. But there was something else. En route south Washington would stop off at his beloved Mt. Vernon. He hadn't seen the plantation for six long years. The visit would be brief, but it was better than nothing. Leaving Mt. Vernon, he would rejoin his army and push on toward Yorktown.

Galloping along the dusty road, Washington was in good spirits and confident of victory. By virtue of numbers alone he should emerge the winner. The allies could call on about eighteen thousand men; the enemy had fewer than seven thousand.

Detail. General Benjamin Lincoln rode forward on his white horse to act as Washington's deputy during the surrender ceremony at Yorktown. Yale University Art Gallery

What's more, the French controlled the Chesapeake. The Royal Navy had recently sailed south from New York in an effort to rescue Cornwallis. An important sea battle took place off the Virginia Capes. The French were victorious, and the British fleet was sent scudding back to its base. Cornwallis was truly on his own.

After a long hard journey Washington and Rochambeau arrived in the field. They were greeted by an enthusiastic Lafayette. Although the marquis hadn't beaten Cornwallis, he had kept him from escaping. Now, with Washington on the scene, His Lordship would really have to worry. Other officers to converge on the allied camp were second-in-command Benjamin Lincoln, "Mad" Anthony Wayne, artillery wizard Henry Knox. Young Alexander Hamilton was there and old Baron von Steuben.

The allies set to work drawing siege lines around the British defenses. They dug entrenchments and built protecting walls. Each day

50

found their advance trenches closer and closer to the British works. Each day found the British position weaker and weaker.

Sealed in from the sea by an enemy fleet, surrounded by enemy troops, Cornwallis was in a desperate situation. His only chance was to stand firm until reinforcements could reach him—when or how he scarcely knew.

All during September he waited and hoped. At the same time, he wrote urgent letters to his superior in New York. Sir Henry Clinton, the new commander-in-chief, promised to send help. The navy would make another foray south as soon as possible. Meanwhile Cornwallis felt he must do everything possible to conserve manpower. After some serious thinking he made a decision, and it was the wrong one. He abandoned two advance redoubts. The allies immediately took over these forts, manning them with crack French and American gunners. The ring was closing. For the defenders of Yorktown it was the beginning of the end.

On October 9 the actual siege began. Like a thunderclap the allies opened fire on the British works. Mortar shell and round shot whizzed through the tall pines, ripped up the sandy soil. Gun emplacements were demolished, houses were levelled. A prime target was Cornwallis' headquarters. The lovely old house was soon a shambles. Undaunted, the earl set up a command post at the back of the property.

The bombardment continued for more than a week. The regulars and Hessians put up a brave fight, but casualties were mounting and ammunition was running low.

With the cannonade at its height Cornwallis wrote Clinton:

My situation here becomes very critical; we dare not show a gun to their old batteries, and I expect their new ones will open tomorrow morning. Experience has shown that our fresh earthen works do not resist their powerful artillery, so that we shall soon be exposed to an assault in ruined works, in a bad position, and with weakened numbers. . . .

At this point Cornwallis conceived a daring plan. The army would break out of Yorktown by boat. They would cross the York River to the Gloucester side, then march northward through Virginia and Maryland and into Pennsylvania. It would mean braving the perils of unknown territory with the enemy surely at their heels. Great courage and boldness would be required, but neither Cornwallis nor his men had ever lacked those qualities.

As night fell over the broad river, the first boats began to push off from the bank. In the beginning everything went well. The men made good progress. Soon they would be out of their terrible predicament and on their way to freedom.

Suddenly a storm blew up. The troops became drenched under a deluge of pelting rain. They were buffeted by driving winds. Thunder and lightning filled the sky and mingled with the fury of the enemy cannonade. The men worked with all their might but could make no headway. For every yard gained, two yards were lost. After hours of toil the weary troops returned to shore and to their embattled fortress.

All night the bombardment continued. A hundred guns went full blast. They thundered against wall and rampart. The peninsula trembled under the impact. It was a one-sided battle. The British were unable to return the fire; their ammunition was exhausted. They could only retreat farther and farther into their defenses. By morning Cornwallis knew what he must do.

The decisive siege of the Revolution was over.

The surrender ceremony took place two days later. For the allies it was a time of high excitement. Eagerly they formed up along the road near the battered British works. The French were resplendent in white coats with gold lace and fancy braid. Facing them across the road stood the Continentals. They too were in uniform, boots and buttons shining. The militia were less martial in leather breeches and fringed hunting shirts.

As the bright autumn sun beamed down on the dramatic scene, a red-coated officer could be seen approaching from the direction of the town. Cornwallis surely. But no. As the man came closer the allies realized their error. It was General Charles O'Hara of the Guards. With head high and eyes forward, the Irishman guided his splendid white horse between the two lines of troops. Whatever emotions he felt were kept to himself. His face seemed carved out of stone.

At the end of the line O'Hara paused. He moved toward a group of allied officers assembled nearby. They too were on horseback. O'Hara addressed General Washington. Briefly he explained that he was Cornwallis' second-in-command. His Lordship was ill and could not attend.

The Virginian was gracious—but deputy should surrender to deputy. He motioned toward his own second-in-command. Benjamin Lincoln rode forward. As O'Hara presented his sword, Lincoln courteously declined it. He then gave instructions for the withdrawal of the defeated troops. The garrison was to file out of Yorktown carrying their arms and equipment. Their colors must be cased, not flying. Regimental bands could play if they chose.

And so as the King's men marched past the allied ranks to become prisoners of war, fifes and drums were playing. The slow solemn tune was called "The World Turned Upside Down." For the British army in America it was exactly that—the world turned upside down.

52

A Soldier's Farewell

The Resignation of General Washington at Annapolis

The war was over, really and truly over. There would be no more battles, no more perilous marches, no snowy camp-sites or cold and hungry comrades looking to him for leadership. General Washington found it hard to believe. Jogging along on horseback, attended by his aides, he gave a weary smile. At long last he could hang up his sword, put away his uniform and become a private citizen again. "Farmer Washington" he liked to call himself, and now his thoughts turned to Mt. Vernon. The lovely plantation on the Potomac beckoned like a light in the darkness. It was December 19, and the general hoped to be home in time for the holidays. Surrounded by family and friends, it would be a merry Christmas indeed.

Eight years before, Washington had left Mt. Vernon to go to the aid of his country. It was the spring of 1775, and the Virginia planter was a delegate to the Second Continental Congress, then meeting in Philadelphia. As he expected, Congress was absorbed in the difficulties with England. It was apparent to all that a full-scale war was in the offing. They must raise an army and find a commander to lead it. This posed a problem. There were many experienced soldiers in the colonies, all eager for the assignment. Whom should they choose? Lawyer John Adams, never afraid to speak up, took the floor. He suggested the name of "a gentleman from Virginia who is among us here and well known to all of us. . . ." Sam Adams seconded his cousin's recommendation. As a result, George Washington, Esq., was duly elected "to command all the continental forces, raised, or to be raised, for the defence of American liberty . . ."

A colonel in the French and Indian War, Washington had long been a member of the Virginia legislature. Both as a soldier and civilian he was held in the highest regard. It was obvious to his colleagues that he was the man for the job. The candidate himself was not so sure. Accepting his commission, he said he felt unequal to the task but resolved to do his best no matter what the cost. "I will enter upon the momentous duty," he promised, "and exert every power I Possess . . . for the Support of the glorious Cause."

From that day forward Washington put aside all personal interests. Unselfishly he devoted himself to the army under his command. And a poor ragtag army it was in the beginning. For all their zeal and patriotism, the soldiers encamped outside Boston that summer were not very military. They had done well at Bunker Hill, but Bunker Hill was only one battle.

The newly made general quickly took stock of the situation. There was much to be done and no time to lose. He rolled up his sleeves and set to work. With the help of his staff, he trained the men; he drilled them; he taught them discipline. In time he had a good fighting force.

Over the years and against fearful odds Washington kept his men together. He led them in victory and defeat, and sometimes there seemed to be nothing but defeat. Long Island, Fort Washington, the retreat across New Jersey. During the darkest days Washington was never far from his troops. He braved the ice-filled Delaware to surprise the enemy at Trenton. He suffered through the long night march on the Princeton road. He shared the perils of Valley Forge. Cold, hungry and ragged, the regiments seemed doomed during that winter of 1777–78. Only a great general could have saved the day. Washington was that general. By his splendid example he inspired the near-mutinous men. He led them from despair to glory.

The siege of Yorktown was his crowning achievement. On the sandy little peninsula he trapped Cornwallis and the Royal Army of Virginia. The "unbeatable" regulars were forced to surrender to mere colonials. It was a bitter pill.

Yorktown marked the real end of the war, but it was two years before the actual peace treaty was signed. In December, 1783, the enemy finally withdrew from the land. British regulars and German mercenaries, they crowded aboard troopships bound for home. They had suffered much during the struggle, only to lose. It had been a fair fight, however, and, win or lose, they were glad it was over. They raised many a cheer as ships caught the wind and made for the open sea.

The Americans in turn went back to their farms and villages. Free men in a free country, they could live their lives as they saw fit. A king three thousand miles away no longer controlled their fate. Citizens of a brand new nation, they were determined to make it the greatest in the world.

Washington's work was done. He had kept his promise. Through his efforts the "glorious Cause" had triumphed. Now he too could think of home. In his mind's eye he saw Mt. Vernon serene under a blanket of snow.

But first there was something he must do. Congress was then sitting in Annapolis, and the general was scheduled to appear before its members. In the little Maryland capital he would formally resign his commission. He would retire from the army. With a flick of the reins he spurred his horse onward. His companions had a hard time keeping up with him.

Four days later the State House in Annapolis was buzzing with excitement. From the polished oak floor to the handsomely carved ceiling, the atmosphere was one of expectancy. Seated at a table draped in crimson, the members of Congress chatted in low tones. President Thomas Mifflin glanced at the clock in the corner. The hands stood at twelve. Secretary Charles Thomson leafed through his journal, found his place and jotted down the date. December 23, 1783. Presently the door of the great hall flew open. On the threshold stood a tall, familiar figure.

All eyes turned in the direction of General Washington. The commander wore his customary uniform, blue with buff facings. At his side hung a green-hilted sword. His brown hair was powdered and combed straight back. A naturally fair complexion was ruddy from much open-air living. In manner he was serious but not self-important.

Washington was met at the door by the Secretary, who escorted him to the place of honor facing the Congress. The general knew most of the delegates. Some had been his friends since prewar days. Seated before them now, he was impressed by their solemn, thoughtful air.

An ornate gallery commanded one side of the room. It was crowded with spectators. There were women in fine clothes, public servants, prominent citizens, all eager to pay homage to the hero of the Revolution.

President Mifflin opened the proceedings. "The United States," he said, "is prepared to receive your communications."

Washington rose and bowed to the members. In his hand he held his address which he referred to from time to time.

"Mr. President," he began.

John Trumbull
The Resignation of
General Washington
at Annapolis
Yale University Art Gallery

The great events on which my resignation depended having at length taken place; I have now the honor of offering my sincere Congratulations to Congress and of presenting myself before them to surrender into their hands the trust committed to me, and to claim the indulgence of retiring from the service of my country. . . .

I consider it an indispensable duty to close this last solemn act of my Official life, by commending the Interests of our dearest Country to the pro-

56

tection of Almighty God, and those who have the superintendence of them, to his holy keeping.

Here Washington's voice failed. The paper in his hand shook visibly and it seemed he couldn't continue. There was a long silence broken only by the ticking of the clock. At last the speaker recovered his voice and went on.

Detail. Members of Congress listened solemnly to General Washington's brief but eloquent resignation speech. Yale University Art Gallery

Having now finished the work assigned me, I retire from the great theatre of action; and bidding an Affectionate farewell to this August body under whose orders I have so long acted, I here offer my commission, and take my leave of all the employments of public life.

With these words Washington drew his commission from an inside pocket of his coat. He went forward and handed it to President Mifflin. He then stepped back and remained standing while Mifflin spoke.

The United States in congress assembled, receive with emotion too affecting for utterance, the solemn resignation of the authorities under which you have led their troops with success through a perilous and doubtful war. Called upon by your country to defend its invaded rights, you accepted the sacred charge, before it had formed alliance, whilst it was without funds or a government to support you. You have conducted the great military contest with wisdom and fortitude. . . .

Listening to the short but eloquent speech, the members were deeply moved. They felt that no one could have received a finer tribute —or deserved it more. George Washington was one of those unusual heroes—a man appreciated in his own time no less than by generations to come.

At the end of the ceremony the Virginian shook hands with each of the members. He spoke to them briefly, for he was a man of few words. What he did say, however, was warm and heartfelt and not easily forgotten. Years later those present still cherished the memory of the dignified commander, in uniform for the last time, as he solemnly said goodbye.

When it was all over, Washington quickly left the hall. Outside, his mount was waiting, restless in the crisp winter air. The former general was soon in the saddle and on his way. At the main road he turned his horse's head in the direction of Mt. Vernon.

George Washington, private citizen, would be home for Christmas.

Index

$#4.95$